W9-BTL-568

Hero Girls

By Annie Buckley

The Child's World
www.childsworld.com

Published in the United States of America by The Child's World®
P.O. Box 326 • Chanhassen, MN 55317-0326
800-599-READ • www.childsworld.com

ACKNOWLEDGMENTS

The Child's World®: Mary Berendes, Publishing Director

Produced by Shoreline Publishing Group LLC
President / Editorial Director: James Buckley, Jr.
Designer: Tom Carling, carlingdesign.com
Cover Art: Slimfilms
Copy Editor: Beth Adelman

Photo Credits:
Cover—AP/Wide World (main and lemonade), Photos.com.
Interior—AP/Wide World: 6, 29; Corbis: 7; Getty Images: 10; iStock:
5, 12, 15, 17, 21, 23, 25; Mission Health Care: 14; Save Our Streams:
19; Photos.com: 27

LIBRARY OF CONGRESS CATALOGING-IN-PUBLICATION DATA

Buckley, Annie.
  Hero girls / by Annie Buckley.
    p. cm. — (Girls rock!)
  Includes bibliographical references and index.
  ISBN 1-59296-744-2 (library bound : alk. paper)
 1. Girls—Psychology—Juvenile literature. 2. Girls—Conduct of
life—Juvenile literature. 3. Women heroes—Juvenile literature. I.
Title. II. Series.
  HQ777.B83 2006
  305.23082'0973—dc22
                              2006001641

CONTENTS

AN INSTANT
Hero

What does the word "hero" mean to you? A firefighter carrying a baby from a burning building? A police officer catching a criminal? Rescue workers saving animals from a flood? They're heroes, all right! They risk their lives to help others. But people can be heroes in lots of other ways, too—even without risking their lives. They see something that needs to be done—and they *do* it.

Some people are heroes even when they're young. They earn respect by overcoming challenges, solving problems, or doing things that make a difference. Let's meet some girl heroes!

You don't have to be world famous to be a hero! Lots of kids do heroic things right in their own neighborhoods.

Here's Bethany Hamilton showing her skill before her accident. She was one of the top surfers in the country in her age group.

Bethany Hamilton lives in Princeton, on the island of Kaua'i, in Hawai'i. In most ways, she's just like other kids—she has dreams for the future and likes to hang out with her friends. One thing Bethany especially loves is surfing. When she was only 13, she was one of the world's best.

That's not what makes Bethany a hero. That's just the start of her story.

On Halloween morning in 2003, Bethany went surfing with her friends, just like any other day. But that day, something happened that changed her life. While she was waiting for a wave, a 14-foot (4-m) tiger shark swam under her surfboard and attacked.

Shark attacks are rare, but they can be deadly. A tiger shark like this one attacked Bethany. Tiger sharks are one of the sharks most likely to attack people.

The shark bit off Bethany's arm, but friends got her to shore and helped save her life. Her friends were heroes, too! Bethany spent some time in a hospital, but less than a month later, she was back on her surfboard.

After the accident, Bethany

Another Athletic Hero

Laurie Stephens of Massachusetts was born with a condition called *spina bifida*. She was unable to walk, but she didn't let that stop her! She learned to ski using a special seat and soon became a very skilled skier. In 2006, she won two gold medals at the Paralympic Winter Games.

could have given up surfing. Instead, she chose to continue. Her courage and strength were an **inspiration** to people all over the world.

Back on her board, Bethany was the 2005 national champion in the Explorer division.

After surviving the shark attack, Bethany was determined to keep following her dreams. Her story made her famous, and part of what makes her a special hero is how she decided to use her fame. She decided to teach people about survival, hope, and courage. She wrote a book called *Soul Surfer*. She also chose to put some of her time, energy, and fame toward helping other kids with physical challenges.

Bethany has taught people to never give up, to have hope, and to be the best they can be every day. Everyone can learn from her courage and her ability to stay positive.

Helping Others Help

In partnership with World Vision's "Put Hope in Motion" program, Bethany has raised thousands of dollars for children with physical challenges. In this program, young athletes help raise money for children in need. World Vision is an international Christian group that helps children and families in many countries. Bethany is using her story to help people around the world!

MAKING A
Difference

Heroic kids come in all shapes and sizes. Some, like Bethany, become famous for their courage. Other hero kids do things that touch people's lives.

What do most heroes have in common? Their **attitude**. When heroes are faced with challenges or bad experiences, they choose to do the best they can. Instead of asking "Why me?", they ask "What can I do?" Instead of getting stuck on what has gone wrong, they look at what they can make right.

OPPOSITE PAGE
Just being a good older sister can be the start of becoming a hero. Are these girls practicing to be doctors—and heroes—when they grow up?

Suzie Tipton has overcome challenges and put her ideas and knowledge to use helping others.

Meet Suzie Tipton from West Virginia. Suzie has **cerebral palsy**, a condition in which she needs a wheelchair to get around. Suzie has put her energy into making medical gear available to other kids with challenges.

Suzie knows what a difference the right medical equipment can make!

In 2003, she came up with a great idea—starting a "loan closet" where kids could **donate** medical equipment as they outgrew it. Then other kids could borrow the equipment that they needed instead of having to buy it.

Special equipment like this electric scooter can really be a help to some kids with physical challenges. It can also be very expensive to buy.

Suzie couldn't start the program alone. The Mission Health Care Foundation in North Carolina provided a **grant** to get Suzie's Closet going. They also provided a place to keep the equipment until it was repaired and ready to use.

Butterfly Award

In 2004, Suzie won the first Butterfly Award from Volvo for life Awards. The award goes to kids who do good things for others even though they face challenges themselves. It honors Alexandra Scott, a young cancer patient whose lemonade stand started a movement that has raised over $5 million for kids with cancer.

Other people gave money and time to help Suzie's Closet grow. Since the program began, it has helped dozens of kids with many different kinds of special needs.

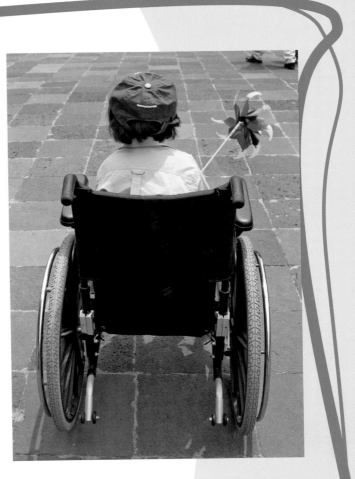

Thanks to Suzie's Closet, many kids now have the gear they need.

Suzie keeps thinking of new ways of carrying on her work. Recently, she held a concert to raise money for kids who must travel to get special medical care.

Suzie Tipton is a great example of someone becoming a hero by helping other people. Three Ohio girls became heroes in another way—by working to clean up their local environment.

Evin McMullen, Angela Primbas, and Amanda Weatherhead learned in school that fish in two local streams were dying. Why? Because the water was too dirty. The fish were brook trout, which need cool, clear water in which to live.

The girls learned everything they could about the fish and the streams. They learned that the dying trout were an important sign of water problems. The girls formed a group called Save Our Stream (SOS) to help fix the situation.

Evin, Angela, and Amanda pose with their teacher at a display about their award-winning project.

The group began working hard to educate people in the community and get them to help. They explained how important the streams were, and how it was in everyone's best interests to keep them clean.

It turned out that people could do lots of things to help—such as not pouring **toxins** down storm drains that emptied into the streams. The group even made SOS T-shirts and hats to help spread the word about their work.

The girls and the group they started made a big difference in their community! In 2004, they won a President's Environmental Youth Award for their effort.

Keeping local streams clean and safe for fish—and people—was the goal of the three Ohio friends.

Two sisters in Denver, Colorado, won an award for helping in a different way. Estephania and Esperanza Chavez started a program to help kids do better in school.

When they were young, the sisters spent time in both Mexico and Colorado before the family finally settled in Colorado. Changing schools and communities was hard. So was switching between Spanish and English. The girls learned that their Denver school was doing poorly on tests compared to

other Colorado schools. They decided to help. They thought, "Why not get older kids to help younger ones?"

The girls got a grant to start Project **Literacy**, in which middle-school students act as **tutors** to help younger students with their reading and writing. The program has been a real success!

Do you know any younger kids that you might help? Being a hero is as easy as helping someone learn.

EVERYDAY
Heroes

The hero girls you've just met have been in newspapers and on television. They've received awards. Their courage has inspired many people.

But you don't have to be famous or win an award to be a hero. In fact, some of the biggest heroes receive no recognition. They might go to your school, live in your neighborhood, or be

part of your own family. They might not even say much about what they've done. But they're people who have made a difference.

Are there any heroes in your life? Are there people you look up to? You can learn a lot from them!

Can a teacher be a hero? Of course! Then you can become your own hero by sharing the talents you learn from the teacher.

If you'd like to volunteer for a good cause, there are plenty of groups in your community that could use your help. Your parents, your school, or your local library can probably point you in the right direction.

How can *you* be a hero? There are opportunities all around you. Have you ever helped younger kids with their homework? Or held a door open for someone carrying groceries? There are more ways to be a hero than you might think. How? By helping out when you see a problem.

Many people become heroes by **volunteering** their time, their knowledge, their skills, or their money to help people or animals in need. Try volunteering your time for a good cause! It feels good, and it's a great way to be a hero. You could read to younger children or help an elderly person.

Look for a hero in your family—maybe it's Grandma!

Is there something you're good at or know a lot about? Perhaps music, or math, or gardening, or soccer, or crafts? Maybe you could be a hero by sharing your knowledge with someone who would love to learn. Or maybe you could use your talents to bring happiness to people—like playing music for other people to enjoy.

Or maybe you could be a hero by helping to raise money for good causes, like some of the hero girls in this book. Even a lemonade stand

When life give you HURRICANE

KIDS WHO CARE MAKE LEMONADE

Kids Who Care

or a car wash or a bake sale can make a difference! And making a difference can be very satisfying.

After all, being a hero isn't about getting rich or famous. It's about doing the right thing.

Gracie Brandt, 10, and her friends in Chicago had a lemonade stand to raise money to help others.

GLOSSARY

attitude   the way you think or feel about something

cerebral palsy   a medical condition that affects parts of the brain that control muscle movement and speech

donate   give something without expecting anything in return

grant   a gift of money that is to be used in a certain way

inspiration   something that fills people with feelings or ideas or encourages them to do something

literacy   the ability to read and write

toxins   chemicals or materials that can be poisonous to humans, animals, or the earth

tutors people who give private lessons to students or help them one-on-one

volunteering offering something, such as your time, without being asked or getting paid

FIND OUT MORE

BOOKS

Earth Book for Kids: Activities to Help Heal the Environment
by Linda Schwartz
(Learning Works, Santa Barbara, CA) 1990
This book includes activities that help kids study the environment and learn about environmental problems.

Girls Who Rocked the World: Heroines from Sacagawea to Sheryl Swoopes
by Amelie Welden
(Beyond Words Publishing, Hillsboro, OR) 1998
Read stories of well-known women who have made an impact.

Sadako and the Thousand Paper Cranes
by Eleanor Coerr
(Puffin Books, New York) 1999
This is the true story of a Japanese girl who helped create a peace movement after World War II.

Soul Surfer: A True Story of Faith, Family, and Fighting to Get Back on the Board
by Bethany Hamilton, with Sheryl Berk
(MTV Books, New York) 2004
This is surfer Bethany Hamilton's story in her own words.

WEB SITES

Visit our home page for lots of links about girls and women doing amazing things: www.childsworld.com/links

Note to Parents, Teachers, and Librarians: We routinely check our Web links to make sure they're safe, active sites—so encourage your readers to check them out!

INDEX

ANNIE BUCKLEY is a writer, artist, and mentor teacher who lives in Los Angeles. She is the author and illustrator of the *The Kids' Yoga Deck* and coauthor of *Once Upon a Time: Creative Writing for Kids*. Annie has taught in grades K–10, and she especially enjoys working with new teachers.